Pine Needles From the Valley of the Pines (1960) [Miscellaneous Works]

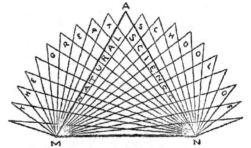

The Philosophy of Individual Life

Pine Needles

From

THE VALLEY OF THE PINES

By

Joseph A. Sadony

The Valley of the Pines

HAPPY is the man
Who knows neither his own weight, strength
Nor destiny.
But whose emotions awaken
At every turn of the road.
Who enjoys a life-long time of appreciation,
With every aspiration guarded.
Who spends his interest on inheritance,
And at death's door finds his capital
Of soul untouched.
That man is a man
Who follows in the shadow of the Master.

The man who has a purpose in life,
Who lives in silence,
Who visualizes no other,
Will surely attain it.
He is poised on his toes,
He is ever ready to spring,
His patience and silence in waiting are his greatest activity.

Don't let your memory of past failure or discord
Swerve you from your set purpose of possibilities still unborn.
Forget by remembering future possibilities.
Think only of success,
And not only will you feed it,
But you will starve failure.

3

You can deform education and music,
But simplicity of purpose is like a large reservoir
With water gates made of concrete and steel
To allow only enough water to pass through
To harmonize with Nature's progress of production and consump-
    tion,
That it may neither run dry,
Nor become a flood to destroy.

The man who labors in silence and darkness
Possesses more power
Than he who holds high his hand in broad daylight
And proclaims his intentions.

In everything that appears good, you may find bad.
A gun may protect you, also kill you.
A knife has its use for or against you.
Electricity may be your servant, and also destroy you.
Food can give health, also sickness.
Small-pox virus may make you immune, but too much will cause
    your death.
Too much of any good thing will destroy your equilibrium, your
    physical poise, or mental balance.
Your body is supposed to represent the earth
In all its parts, harmoniously, in beauty and strength;
The most enduring, artistic, graceful, compact, complete mansion
Where the soul may live as the King of the Earth.

If you play fair,
Regardless how you lose, you win.
You may have a poor partner to make you lose today;
But tomorrow you will have a better partner than you are,
Who will win for you what you lost today—
Just because you were or would have been a good loser,
Having done the best you could.

The more strings you find to the human harp,
The greater your song of emotions, happiness, and success.
  So search for each string hidden.
See to it that it is tuned correctly.
Then you may hear every song ever sung.
You need but to listen,
And each mental faculty will vibrate its secret of life.
Listen only, for your voice can only repeat,
And you will know why the wise men are often silent.
They are listeing to the voice of growth, life, and God's message.
Do you envy the success of others;
Complain at your misfortune?
If so, bear in mind that there is no living thing
That must not work in darkness of the mines.
Even the Embryo of the life within its prison walls of shell or flesh,
The roots of flowers and trees,
Man in the dark ages of ignorance.
He digs up his metal for swords and plowshares, locks and powder.
If he fails to wear a crown that fits him,
It was then like the tree that complained that it failed to blossom,
Because it did not labor among its roots to produce them,
Let alone the fruits longing to follow the blossoms unto life.

When God can trust His creation
He will place in Man's hand
A most precious power
To create what he will.
And when Man realizes this
He will have burned out
All inclination to do wrong.

Often men think they are making great progress
Because their feet carrying big loads run swiftly;
But are blind to the fact that they are in a revolving squirrel cage
    getting nowhere;
And the man sincere, working daily, sees no progress
Because he is travelling on the large ship of Progress, unaware.

It is not enough that we write a letter.
We must have the address, buy a stamp and mail it.
It is not enough to love.
We must repay.
Not enough to earn money.
We must spend it well.
Not enough to pray.
We must give prayer muscle to attain.
It is not enough to possess a steel bar to make a compass,
We need a prayer of magnetism to discern.
A prayer is but to tune in so we may realize a duty of Nature.
To show us the land-marks to obey a law
That we might live right, according to that which created our
    being and consciousness.
Our prayer is but a hammer to the chisel,
Hope to faith, internal light in the dark nights of doubt and des-
    pair.
It is the birth of hope
That faith may lead us to its realization,
To admit a supreme Being,
A law greater than our conception,
To recognize a power we must obey,
A wall of obedience; a recipe,
Directions to attain that which will fill a vacuum,
A felt want to complete an Ideal.

Calamities and misfortunes are but brakes applied to your
    freight train going down your montainside;
Or sand thrown across the path of your sled that has no
    brakes,
In order to slow up your speed,
So you may reason why and where you are going to land,
    before it is too late.
Nature uses this means of vaccination while still in your
    prime
And strong enough to avoid and withstand the vicissitudes
    of life.

Don't condemn a fool for lack of wisdom.
He is at least contented,
While a man of wisdom may be happy,
But the law of adjustment gives him a personal responsibility,
Which prevents what constitutes the contentment of a fool.

Try to remember everything
On your journey up the mountain of life,
So that when you glide coasting down
You may know what to do, and avoid,
In order to complete your life successfully.

If your mind is not in your exercise,
Your heart not in your love,
You are but putting a losing, useless drain upon your energy—
A false hope in your Ideals.

No man need envy another.
Nature has so constructed its laws
That each man may create and live in a world of his own;
And as with the stars of heaven,
Need injure none by contact, though living in one mansion.

Do not fear to do wrong.
Fear rather that you might fail
To do good.
Do not think you have lost,
What you have never found.
For there is nothing ever lost,
Or ever found.
If we have "found",
It belongs to another.
If we have "lost",
It was never ours.

We still have more to learn
Of the rooms of man's mind,
To find the doors leading to that religious ecstacy,
The mystery, the frenzy of the aborigines,
The bliss of divinity felt by martyrs and saints,
The hypnotic power of our professional men—
All still in its infancy.
Who shall dare to ridicule or challenge unknown facts,
The vehicle which led the human race to absolute facts,
The few that we have,
Still, self-evident.
Can we not be charitable enough
To believe men sincere in their own honest convictions?
Time will prove a greater power in man's mind
Than we have thus far admitted.

You may assume vows before the eyes of men,
But the vows before the eye of your soul
Are more sacred and binding by your conscience than any others.

Every man and woman is placed in a melting pot of life,
Sorted according to his ambition.
The fire of experience either burns them to dross
Or purifies to achieve.
He who possesses character need not fear the flame of elimination;
But those who have cause to fear are but returned to whence fear
    lost confidence.
They are depreciated for their assumed credit.
For every plant there grows an affinity
Upon which it may live and thrive,
Be it food or love, to destroy or to save.

The Valley of the Pines

IN trying to make the world better
 By making others obey your will and opinion,
 Why not make yourself obey
And let the example show its effect?
And each be a captain of his own ship,
So that the human inclination of the "masses" will do likewise,
Steering it safely,
Instead of one mortal trying to do so,
Which is impossible.

♠

Whenever you wish to do something,
No matter what it might be,
Think twice—
The day thought and the night thought,
The result to others,
And the result to yourself.
It will astonish you
What an interesting game you may play
During the rest of your life.

♠

It's time ill spent
To labor for the approbation of acquaintances.
In the final reckoning
You shall receive only criticism
For your pains.
The Evil will condemn your efforts,
Because of your patience with good.
And the Good
Will question
Your pity for Evil.

The time a person really suffers tortures is when he has sympathy for those in pain or sorrow.

Try to learn to think what you want to think, that will bring happiness. Then see the attitude of your emotions. your faith and the results. Thoughts come first; regret or action next, and if the latter, happiness results.

Do you think your body is the only place you can live in? If so, tell me where you are in your dreams, far from home?

Half of the time you did not mean what you said to hurt. It was but habitual, and you felt the stronger of the two .So go easy not to let things slip over the tongue that you may regret and never make good.

Is not the simple life the best
After all?
Is there much to be gained
By responsibilities and fame?
Do they strengthen our hearts and love?
Or do they honor our egotism
And inflame our pride?
The more we acquire,
The more a slave to circumstances
We are apt to become—
Until we may not call our soul our own.

If I offer you an epigram you cannot digest,
Then I have given you something of value.
And you find that your sharp knife
Of discrimination
Is still in your hand,
And rust is not blunting the cutting edge.
  Real joys are debts paid in full.

Don't try to think with your brain when that brain is not normal—
Causing thoughts not normal.
Is it not like a tired body which cannot raise an arm?
Why expect a tired brain to do more?
Surely you ought to know when a straight line is made crooked,
As well as when a circle is made straight,
And realize that if you know the difference,
The knowing is proof of an inborn, independent justice,
A knowledge of a moral law,
A conscience of set rule, wrong and right, top or bottom, cold or hot.
Our own law of cause and effect adjusts our judgment
As to what is the cause, and what is the effect,
Whether standing on our feet, or walking on our hands.

Often when you turn off the light, you find you can't sleep.
Well, then keep the light on and try to keep your eyes open. You will
fall asleep, because you are seeing with your eyes. But when dark,
you see with your thoughts, and that keeps you awake. I've tried
it, and I'm no better than you are; and perhaps no worse.

No man can hope in one life
To complete great achievements.
He can expect to accomplish
Only that which is himself.
He may build the greatest ship
But fail to see it launched.
Plan the greatest city
For his children to build and complete.
Paint the greatest picture
For age to illuminate.
But he may build a ladder
Which by the aspiration of his Soul
Will reach into heaven.

Don't despair at your slow growth as roots of an oak tree.
The more slowly you grow, and the more sure of yourself,
The greater will be your tree that will be supported by your long
    development.
Don't mind those plants that mature over night—
They eat, and live only for the next day.
Do you expect so short a life?
It requires but twenty-one days to hatch a chicken egg.
What about a goose, and how long does it live?
You must pay the fiddler by the hour,
Not by the tune.
Are not the limbs of the coming oak,
Yes, even the leaves, predestined as to their respective position on
    that tree
Within that small acorn, as the nerves and arteries within the
    embryo of man
To designate its species?

Does thought give you pleasure?
If not, is not anticipation a part of the realization?
And if true, why not create more thought of happiness
To hasten the ambitions of your heart—?

Your strength is judged by those who love you,
Your reputation by those who don't.

Periodically in history the ground of man's mind is plowed under,
    everything apparently uprooted into uncertainty. How else
    shall the old habits of thought be broken up to clear the way for
    a new epoch?

He is only successful who, after having attained his goal, re-
    members his friends who see in him the same friend of old,
    whose success has not stained nor embittered him.

A doctor can help you live
As long as there is still a tension on your main spring;
But if that has run down,
No matter how good the works and jeweled settings,
Don't expect him to do what God and Nature has forbidden.
The main spring absorbs that which it gives up,
Regardless of the value of the works,
Which in turn must be kept in good condition
Or there will be that pull of the spring still there
To work, escape, or be placed in another rundown clock in good
    repair:
All created to tell us of wasted time
That might have been used in knowing all these things
To lengthen opportunities and happiness.
See a good jeweller occasionally,
If your clock goes too slow;
And a minister of the gospel to get the correct time,
And a doctor to set and clean the work.

If you have made a mistake,
Why not backtrack
Just to convince yourself how it happened,
And save a lot of good wasted self-pity
Making your next mistake in thinking people believe your alibi.

Do you believe,
Because you can afford the life of ease,
That it exempts you from labor,
When labor is so essential for physical strength,
To support the mental wealth by its personal responsibility?
If your eyes fail to wake up your soul
By the display of beauty ond art,
Your ears, as sensitive as they may be,
Shall be deaf to all music, melody, and words of love,
For seeing, hearing, tasting, and feeling enter different doors,
But into one room only.

It is useless to worry over what cannot be helped.
And what cannot be helped calls for action,
Not worry.
Worry saps vitality.
And renders one unfit for the action
Necessary to make conditions better.

When you think yourself greater
Than your brother man,
Remind yourself of those things
That you did ungraciously and unwell.

Prayer is but a cup to be filled,
An appeal to the unknown, and not an order,
Not a demand for that which we ourselves may do or reason.
It is to tune in, to strengthen hope unto faith,
That patient path that leads to what we prayed for,
A telescope to see; a microscope to discern.

If you have a just reason to become angry,
And keep it under control,
You punish your enemy.
But if you give way to it,
Your anger punishes you.

How often have we not been let down, forsaken, depressed
in spirit. But how do we know that it isn't a test of our sincerity
of purpose and worthiness in overcoming adversity when in our
power to do so? Has this not perhaps been given us as an honor of
trust by Him who gave us life and individuality to rise above it
all and achieve reward for efforts made?

It's not what you do when you are busy that counts most.
It is what you do when you are idle that makes or breaks you.

If you fail to make good, and do not know why,
Have you ever stopped to think
That it might be a childish dream of fear, petrified,
Which still remains with you, unconsciously?
Have you ever stopped to think that our anger and disappointment
Magnify more by our unreasonable selfish imagination
Than that which first caused our anger,
So easy then to forgive,
Until we have added our own subtle poison of disappointment or
false pride?

Most of us are becoming blind to today's opportunity
Which might shape tomorrow's success.
Instead, we but hope for tomorrow's success;
And fail because of today's neglect.

The spirit of serving is becoming
To the high
As well as the lowly.
But dignity belongs to him
Who is able to uphold it.

Few of us think real thought.
We only think we think,
It is all Vanity in new forms.
One must be alone to think,
Uninfluenced by the world's desires.

Don't be too hasty to collect your first week's wages;
Neither expect a silver cup at your first attempt.
Be glad for the attempt.
Victory and silver cups follow always.
If you still have faith after your first three prayers were answered,
You may be sure your recommendation is being placed on record.
To deliver goods on credit.

There is a limit to man's power of reasoning.
He may be finally able to complete
A jig-saw puzzle,
In a fashion according to the
Number of blocks he has found
Through his efforts to excel.
But in his youth it makes no difference
What block he chooses first,
In his attempt to solve the Unknown,
He will but reach a plane of incompleteness,
Until each block of life's problems
Has been found, and properly placed.
And when he reaches that point of evolution,
Man's understanding may, perhaps,
Partake somewhat of completeness and universality.

Daily contact with an enemy results in the enemy being despised.
But if he is avoided, he creates another weapon to hurt in his
    absence.
The farther removed the more horrible the cry of the battlefield . . .
Problems and misfortunes are blessings of immunity to oblivion
    and failure.
They awaken and excercise a sluggish brain.
They strengthen faith and hope born in the Soul.
But if sorrows and calamities go by unnoticed,—if no lesson has
    been learned, then a life has been in vain.
How can we enjoy without having known sorrow?
How can we know sorrow without joy?
Sympathy is born in sorrow.
Appreciation often dies in joy.
But the memory of both sorrow and joy awakens faith, hope and
    charity, consideration, kindness and love.

The Valley of the Pines

THERE are sorrows which time alone can cure
By what light we find appertaining to Eternity.
When we deliberately lose one eyelid, we do not destroy the
light,
But only shut it from our own view:
That light which but reflects itself, lends its truth,
Brings out the soul of that which it touches.
So keep your eyes open.
At best they see but dimly.

The last stroke of the bell
Tells the time.
The others tell only part of the truth.

Live right and you will act right.
Act right, and you will have to think right.

Things are only beautiful when you are in tune with them.
If you are not, then tune yourself in.
It may be your fault.

To improve the future,
Review the past.
Our sorrows are receipts for debts paid.
Our good deeds are negotiable checks.

The see-saw of life must be kept balanced,
For such is the law.
But ever upon the end that is high up
Will I throw my weight
For the sake of your Soul.
If you have lifted high
And dragged down the clouds from
Where they belong,
And walk the earth, half-dazed
In a spiritual mist,
While the good feet of your body
Dangle helpless,—
Do not think me cruel
If I demand red blood where red blood is needed.
And if I tell you
That well-prepared food, and care of the body,
Are as important for the Soul
As are thoughts of God.

It is the value you place on your interest for tomorrow that
gives birth and strength to your hopes and verifies your faith—
and leaves no grounds for fear, apprehension or sorrow.

Who is wrong when a man is accused of a wrong that he
sincerely believes was right, and is then called a liar because it was
a lie to another, but not so to him who honestly believed it to be
the truth? Are they not both to blame for not understanding
each other?

In the name of Charity and Love,
Give your surplus profits in your youth,
So they may be returned to you
In your old age
As necessities.

If you would be safe from
Superstition and spiritual fanaticism
Remain near the shore
Of the stream of life,
Where reason may direct you.
When in the water,
Not to go beyond your depth,
Not to drift upon the running stream,
And to hold you,
When upon the shore,
From wandering out into the desert.

Man is tested only by his faith to endure.

In human experience,
Perhaps the most precious time lost,
The greatest tortures,
The most tears shed,
The greatest cruelties,
Wars and bloodshed,
Have been endured and committed
In the name of a man-shaped God
And (what irony!) called Love.
Humanity has shaped and clothed Him.
Which is as impossible as for a new-born Babe
To support its father by its understanding.
Why? When? And where?
An understanding mind knows that God exists.
Whether we are in His likeness,
Or will be in centuries to come,
Or perhaps at the close of our perfection,
Or never,—
It does not matter.
The great problem that has been,
Is, and ever will be before us,
Is to learn, not *what* to love,—
But *how?*

No one will deny facts, unless he has a subtle purpose to use opportunities for selfish purposes. Truth is self-evident and needs no support. It supports itself. And if the pillars of a structure are lies, it will but collapse. Still, the spirit of true support is ever present, so that a new permanent structure shall rise from the ashes and dust of falsehood. There are ever present health germs to continue life, even among death germs. That is the law of adjustment, compensation and growth, the manifestation of life.

All that matters most to man is back of his eyes, and there he flounders in the dark, thinking he thinks a thought, but unaware of the origin of that thought, or of its fruits; "Imagining" things without the slightest conception of the power and mechanism that he is using.

Do you ever hear or enjoy birds singing?
If not, your judgment is lopsided.
Even your art is deformed,
Or you may be stone deaf.
If the latter, your eyes should hear their song;
For even in a "Depression", Nature sings her song of praise,
Except man, its master, who learns to forget.

I believe it is best to carry a little good timber, and only a few
    first-class tools—having them always ready at hand—than to
    carry many tools and much timber to hew and shape.
Accept from the store of knowledge only that which you actually
    need in life's battle, and no more, or you will be too heavily
    weighted.
It is not the knowledge that is acquired that matters.
It is how it is used.

All life is a labor
Until we love to labor,
And then it is play.

He who is humble with simplicity has a right to it only when he
    has the primitive strength to convince;
Because a coward may be humble, through fear;
A fool, simple through ignorance.
But it requires strength to burn dynamite slowly.

Never defend a fault but prune the evil plant.
To admit it is to pull it up by the the roots.
And if you do, you will have enough strength of character
To profit by it.
Do not let your thoughts run idle. Try to keep them in a channel
    to clothe them so they may live within themselves and bear
    fruit.

Do not be so egotistical as to think
That God has neglected to pick
Some one to fill your place
When you leave this earth,
No matter what your responsibilities
Or what throne you have sat upon.

The good you have done can no more be destroyed
Than an atom annihilated.
You might release power into a new form
But you cannot destroy it
Just because you cannot see it after its transformation.
It is still in existence
As well as our unkind deeds.

Why fight or dispute when there is nothing to fight about?
For the truth still remains, regardless of the outcome.
And truth defends itself.
And the man who fights, loses—even if he wins.

He who lives by the sword
Must not expect mercy when it is shattered.
But he who gives mercy
Need never ask it.

He who carries the atmosphere of nobility about him,
Heals the multitudes merely by his presence.
He frees—never enslaves.
Will-power repels.
He who uses will-power to enslave others
Finds himself enslaved.
The greatest and noblest quality is kindness:
Kindness to all living things.
Life is an individual unfoldment
Which necessitates the constant observance
Of our thoughts, words, deeds.
No other one is so much concerned with them,
As ourselves.
Food that is health-giving to one,
Often brings disease to another.
There are no general set of rules—man made—
For the evolution of mind, soul and body
For all men.
Each must learn to know his own particular force
Of character.
Polarize it,
To time, condition, and locality.
Then can there be no difficulty
In building the Temple.

A man who has the truth
Needs no waste of words to express it.
But he who has no understanding
Must adopt the subterfuge of words
To hold attention, for results expected
That never arrive.

Did you paint your picture of life with regret and failure?
You did this with the best brush and paint you had?
Why not forget your mistake,
And see how easy it is to find a better brush,
And more permanent, slow-drying oil,
So you may correct mistakes,
Or change the color before it hardens
As you did the last picture over night, because you
        thought you might lose the scenery?

If you don't appreciate fine weather as much as you condemn bad weather; if you don't praise good as much as you criticize bad, you are lopsided in your judgment and convict yourself accordingly.

Remember a full stomach today will not satisfy you tomorrow.
This morning's opinions will change by tonight.
Expect your compensation in all you do,
Or your journey will be in vain.
All things here are momentary.
You must catch them on the fly as they pass by.
Tomorrow is unborn. Today is yours.
Yesterday, the skeleton of your efforts made.

No man need envy another.
Nature has so constructed its laws
That each man may create and live in a world of his own;
And as with the stars of heaven,
Need injure none by contact, though living in one mansion.

If all things go wrong do just a little analyzing and find out what
      you are thinking with.
See if it is the same material with which you thought when all
      seemed so bright and happy.

It is not what you think you can do that is convincing,
It is what you already have done, that entitles you to live in
the ranks of the Immortals.

It is not always the brave
Who can exhibit a lot of scars.
Even a careless fool can do that.
But brave men and women have scars deep and livid,
Unseen, deep within their hearts,
And still carry a smile of understanding
With that great character that lives long
After they have passed on.
There are many such people all around you,
Revealed only when catastrophe hovers,
And when real charity and mercy are most in demand,
Then Washingtons and Lincolns are born.

Try to make it difficult to attain what you want
And not only will you be more appreciative and happy,
But permanently contented with your efforts
To just keep warm and comfortable, while others
Are burning up with success or freezing with failure.

When your longings are acute,
You either have something
To give away
Or, something to be filled.
You are either overfed,
Or starving.
You may be rich, yet poor.
Or poor, but wealthy.
Or a poor rich man.

The Valley of the Pines

NEVER climb a mountain that reaches nowhere
And which is more difficult to descend
Then ascend.
The reward of curiosity
Is but to forfeit energy
That might have furthered happiness
And brought joy.
If you have no interest in life,
Reserve your smallest strength
In silence, solitude and rest,
And there will be revealed to you
Your work,
That thoughtlessness and wrong environment
Hid from you.
There is nothing on earth that has life
That does not strive to enlarge,
Beautify, and perpetuate itself
Through desire, vanity and love.

A chosen shepherd should,
And must know of the wolves' habits
As much as what is for the welfare
Of his sheep.
Only then is he a good shepherd.

There is greater virtue in charity shown by the poor than by the
rich, because of the effort made to relieve distress in the
presence of want.

Men may organize the strongest fraternity in the world,
Still Destiny's "fate" orders an individual accounting of each
    official.
None are exempt from judgement, penalty or reward.
As long as someone shall exceed him,
Facts shall be made known, good or evil, gain or loss.
For when we go to our long sleep,
Everything of material value will be emptied from the pockets we
    have worn;
Cash or bonds, worthless or of great value.
So why not do something that will last,
Without regret in the barter of brains and willpower,
So there can be no loss or sorrow
For having done just that thing
That will outlast your name.
Is it so great to have been,
To have had, but not held?
A common thief can steal and hold the sceptor of a king.
So hold only that which is becoming and profitable.
It can be done!

He who strives for Truth,
Though he be ever so great a liar,
Will some time shed his coat
And marvel at his own cleanliness.
No one can strive for an Ideal
Unless God has already planted the seed.
One's ideals advertise one's possibilities.
Be a man, or woman, ever so bad,
There is someone who will recognize
Manhood in him—
    And an Angel in her.

Don't ever try to force intuition, if you expect the truth. You can
    only be impressed by it. You cannot influence or govern it—
    for it comes to you only according to your worthiness, and your
    ability to receive it.

If we wish to make a masterpiece we must have the concept in mind first and then materialize it.

If we use the hardest marble, the best tools, the work will endure though the labor be strenuous.

Under the law of compensation it will pay ...

So with thought!

It is only by deep thinking that we crystalize monuments of endeavors.

If we govern thought it means all desires granted.

Should we realize that attention and concentration upon a given desire will bring the result, discord and sorrow will be lessened.

But always, must we think our own thoughts, and not those of another.

For it is by our own individual thought that we evolve toward perfection.

It is not by the thoughts of others.

They come to us as echoes, which do record in the Soul's memory as our own.

They are reflections, moon-beams, light that passes us by, and is reflected back to us ...

Thoughts are things that record within the Soul as sound upon the record of a victrola.

They are echoes of vibration.

They are irritants to the Soul, as light is to the optic nerve, sound to the inner ear ...

How many people really know how to think?

I see most minds become stimulated by emotion—by objects the eye sees, by feelings of pain, loss or possession.

Few men give thought full sway.

Few broaden out and allow higher influences to stimulate their actions.

Few think to make room for new thoughts, new ideas, and things ...

It is not so much what a man thinks, as how he thinks and what he is capable of thinking ...

Watch a crowd.

Observe the expression on the faces of the people, their actions.

And you will know what thoughts animate them.

You will also know whence they came, and whither they are going.

I have found that we are not tested
For the day only.
The real test comes in years alone.
We pray in the morning
And expect our reward at night,
While the prayer has not yet reached the ceiling
Of our dwelling.
The seed of prayer lives eternally,
And is not governed by seconds.
Often when we pray for something
And the prayer is barely strong
Enough to stand alone,
It will be carried in the arms
Of an Angel to the Master.
And when the creator of this prayer
Has lived his mortal life,
And passes away,
An answer to his prayer
Will be delivered to his children
After his death
As a recognition from God.

No matter how great or important
Is your work,
Be not blind to the smallest things.
For without them, nothing great
Is permanent.
It is the fibers that hold
Together the strongest oak,
Where then is strength?

He who builds a world of his own
Need never leave it for pleasure.
For the entire world outside
Will try to enter
To keep him company.

It is better to master the language of your own efficiency, so you may the better recognize and read your own milestones, than to lose time in deciphering those of your neighbor whose identity lies far from your own.

There are those who must dig and find gold,
Those who cast and shape it,
And those who chase and engrave it for others to wear and use
Thus also must there be Thinkers
Who are inspired to find ideas,
For others to write them,
And still others to express them
For others to use and become happy in the possession of truth.

Many a man would acomplish more in life
If he did not wait
For the approval or flattery of friends.
For when they stop,
Efforts do likewise.
Better that he compete with himself,
As he would in playing solitaire.

A man who excuses
Or defends a lie
Tells two of them.

He who preaches
And does not live it,
Preaches falsely,
No matter what his sermon may be.

He who sets a pace
Must keep it up.
Or he will be crushed by those behind
Who are kept pacing.

Often your thoughts, like your muscles, become tired. Change them, and you will find complete rest and rejuvenation.

Don't be a too self-confident, arrogant student in your class-rom.
Remember that he who gave birth to your lessons
Had to earn his discoveries by hard labor, sacrifices, and
    acknowledgements.
So don't glory in your education
At the price of the humiliation of one
Who has not your opportunities to learn in contented, ideal sur-
    roundings.
You may have to test and prove your findings
In the place where they were born.

Anger may generate courage.
It may also leave cruelty in its place.
Ambition and desire are fire under a steam boiler,
Powder in a rifle,
Without which there can be no successful purpose.

The noblest thoughts and achievements
Are those created when the human heart works in unison
With its Creator.

He who is wise has a right to judge,
But will not.
He who is ignorant has no right
But does, unwisely.
Therefore, why judge?
It is but to admit or betray
Shortcomings or vices.

One often arrives at a blank wall
Dismayed.
And failing to look up,
One does not see the ladder hanging from on high.

The Valley of the Pines

WHAT is worth possessing
Is worth waiting for, and what
Is worth waiting for, is worth possessing.
There is no value to that which has been
Lightly acquired.
It does not represent labor, or even patience,
Hope or love.
Love exists upon love
And willingly carries labor upon its shoulders.

We who would succeed and be happy,
Must first understand discipline,
And live under its rule.

By trying to deceive and fool others,
You are but fooling yourself,
Depriving yourself of the very thing
You are trying to attain.
When you forget how to laugh or play,
It is a sign of danger,
And that the safe cache in the wilderness is being robbed or
    despoiled
Which you must depend upon for sustenance and life
On your way back to complete your life's cycle.
So don't be foolish and deceived,
By gazing into the mirror of your friend's opinion.
Look straight at real life.

No matter how wise your teacher may be,
Remember you use the same tools he does to draw your conclusions.
Your ink of reason may not be so indelible
But if you believe yourself a little more,
Your logic will be self-evident enough not to cheat you, or lead
you astray.
God, through Nature, has seen to that when He gave you your
mental equipment.

Nature is firmly rooted.
Man can change and travel, tuning himself in to his own.
Why do you laugh at things humorous, mostly when tuned
in with association, as in a theater?
Seek that which is a feast to your vision—
Not too much, or you lose perspective.
Not too little, or it does not appease your appetite.

Anyone without exercise soon dies of idleness, as a crippled wolf
in the wilderness.
Give your ears exercise by hearing good music
And see what mental shape you are in to appreciate it.
See if you can hear the call of your soul and heart—
A few words of praise and love,
A command, an inspiration, or your execution.
Give your eyes a little exercise, to see if they recognize land-marks,
Or whether you are lost, and if not,
To see the right from the wrong,
A coming storm, or a friend from a foe.
Give your taste exercise to see if you are eating right food, pure
air, and fragrance.
See if you can sense the soul of the earth and its flowers by their
aroma.
Do these things, and you soon will be active,
Eliminating or absorbing, to give out the fruits
That only such a masterpiece as your body can achieve.
To the betterment of everything that has life,
To prove your own activity, which alone can be life.

Truth is so simple
That children play with it every day
While old men seek it in vain.

Why desecrate this hour of day by fear of disaster;
When that day and hour has already been set?
For even death requires but a moment:
But see how many hours of torture you have made it,
And still are yet to die.

Have you ever analyzed what you really wanted,
And then acquired it, only to find
That you did not need it,
Could not afford it
And could do without it without sacrifices,
Save when possessing it, in keeping it?
How many wants are there to want
But never to possess?
Once in your keeping, you are more unhappy
Than when still wanting them.

What is it to be be happy and contented? Is it to look forward to
    something? To labor to put away for a rainy day that never
    comes? To hoard until there is enough for a cloudburst
    to drown your children?

Much is hidden from those who will not seek.
I often test my friends.
If a grain of truth dropped,
Fails to grow,
I do not repeat the experiment.
It is useless to try to grow certain plants out of season.

We stumble
And knock down the domino ahead of us.
Which knocks down the next ahead,
And that the next,
And so on, till out of sight.
And we soon forget the blunder made,
Until we are awakened
By a blow from behind,
Which knocks us down,—
And discloses the fact
That the dominoes of life
Are arranged in circles.
If we hit one ahead,
We must expect,
Sooner or later,
The blow from behind.

If you think that you have discovered
New Truths,
Do not be in haste
To disclose them.
They will not vanish.
They will grow.
Keep the roots,
And give away the fruit only.

He who prays
Is benefitted more by praying
Than in having his prayer answered.

What picture shall we set in the frame of the mind today?
It is for each one to choose.
Shall it be the picture of yesterday's mistake unfinished,
Or just a new background of tomorrow's masterpiece?

Each mortal has a garden,
An individual responsibility.
You have no right to work in your neighbor's garden,
And so neglect your own.
Neither have you a right to expect
Your neighbor to work in yours,
And influence him to neglect his own.
For all gardens of love hold love, hold loveliness,
Whatever we sow, will grow.

Never seek an inspiration,
Or think of one,
Unless you intend to write it,
Or record it in action of some form.
If you disregard an inspiration
When it is given you,
Then will it disregard you
When you seek it.

If you look at a man and like him
He must be good if you are good.
Your best judgement is your highest standard
Of your individual education.

The future is for you to will and shape.
The present is concrete.
Past, it is gone forever.

Your strength in the chain of life is but the strength of its weakest
link. So test each link before you weld yourself to others, or
your reserve strength will be superfluous while the weaker
feels safe.

The motion of the mind is thought.

And anything whatsoever that gives rise to thought is life-giving.

We all must admit that "as we think, so we are."

We make ourselves what we are by how we think.

If we are not what we want to be, it is our own fault in wrong thinking . . .

A beautiful green meadow covers the unsightly earth of dead resolutions.

Each blade of grass is a monument to the masses.

Each flower reaching into the air is a monument to the genius, the martyr, the man or the woman who dares carry out the aspiration of their souls.

Be happy in the thought that all your possibilities and blessings thus far have not unfolded themselves.

You still have before you a realization beyond your present comprehension.

It is impossible for you to draw a picture which you have not seen unless you make it a composite, using that which is already in memory.

But it requires new actual experiences, and new emotions and new designs which you require from environments, to make you realize greater sensations and joys.

Many times we forget to remember,
But when the waters have been troubled
Let us remember to forget.

Man seldom breaks through the walls
Of his Infancy.
But when he does, he becomes a
Philosopher.
And he sees not the inside of the egg
In which he was born.
But the limitless space
And Eternity.

You know we often think ourselves misunderstood, when it is we
ourselves who misunderstand others.

It is best that we live on the borderline of pain and sorrow that we
may the better realize our duty and our mission. And that we
may be constantly awake to danger.

We must ever avoid too much pain, or we shall become calloused and
heedless of the warning when the limitations of one of Nature's
laws has been reached.

Indeed, that is what pain is, such a warning.

Measure your success
Not by the competitors you have beaten,
But by the new friends that have come to make your
acquaintance.

It is not always the sins we have committed that call us to account
at our maturity; but the virtues we have neglected that demand
and uneasy conscience.

Labor, discipline and self-control still the fire of impulsiveness
so the hand of virtue may lead on to fill the void created by environments contrary to the growth of enlightenment.

The big "sins" we need not fear.
We see them and guard against them.
It is the little germs,
The little seeds and first thoughts
That are unseen
But scattered everywhere
That deserve our greatest attention.

You can only prove friendship by deeds and sacrifices;
Not charity and gifts,
But understanding and loyalty.

Learn the meaning of the word, "Appreciation,"
And half of your faults, sins and disappointments
Will have vanished.

Do you think it an honor
To have brought up a child—
As much as a child
To have given a parent
An *opportunity* to have brought up a child
By the discipline of Personal Responsibility?
So that after all, the score is even,
As fatherhood and childhood.

If you wish to avoid sorrow, then eat and drink of life's joys moderately. Reserve the surplus for the time when you will be hungry and thirsty. Your greatest blessing, misused, can become your greatest curse.

Time your efforts to Success by the clock of Nature. If you wish to live but for a day of splendor, then time yourself by seconds. But if you wish to bloom eternally, then count your efforts by centuries.

Great men forget great things done,
But will weep because they failed to accomplish
What a child is capable of doing.

The Valley of the Pines

THERE are sorrows which time alone can cure
By what light we find appertaining to Eternity.
When we deliberately close one eyelid, we do not
destroy the light,
But only shut it from own own view.
That light which but reflects itself, lends its truth,
Brings out the soul of that which it touches.
So keep your eyes open.
At best they see but dimly.

It is the sculptor who hews the hardest stone,
The writer who uses the most permanent ink,
And the philosopher the most simple truths,
Who rides the tempests and survives the dark ages of time . . .

As we think and act, so are we.
Our thoughts leave an indelible mark upon our features,
While our actions leave monuments
In the graveyards of the memories of others.

An intelligent man fears an ignorant man
Because of that ignorant man's ignorance.
An ignorant man fears an intelligent man
Because of that knowledge the intelligent man possesses which
is unknown to the ignorant.
The suspicions of the ignorant create fear that weakens.
The intelligent man is aware of that weakness,
So is strengthened.

Which plant or bulb in the human garden
Do you water and cultivate most?
What blossoms are most pleasing to you?
Cultivate all,
Until each blooms
To your own satisfaction;
And then you will KNOW
What constitutes your creation.

If you assume the adoption of a child, be sure that you do
your duty as a parent, and it may be a better child to you than your
own, and even teach you how to be a good father or mother.

Obey the simple things of life
And the big things will not overthrow you.
Choose the correct grains of sand,
And the house of bricks will not crumble.
Likewise with an army.

We have been given just so much energy, like money, to spend as
we will, or throw away.
What shall we do with it?

To believe in a God
Is the most perfect principle
To attain perfection.
To imitate a God,
The quickest way to attain that which we seek.
For it is the wish itself
Clothed in reality
Which but strives to manifest itself
Through Faith,
In its own individuality.

I believe that some men
Have been made leaders
And have been given great missions to perform
For Humanity.
And it is far better to give to the man
One pound of sugar
So that he may be better able
To carry out the great work
Than to give to hundreds and thousands
Human beings,
One grain each,
And have all lost.

We are all too close to our labor and acquaintances
To see truthfully as things really are.
Just widen the space and see for yourself.

If your education does not give you contentment,
    happiness, confidence, and success,
        You have been cheated.
And that by yourself.

Life and history repeat themselves constantly.
Go count your cycles, that you may improve, and profit by your
    mistakes.

A fool, on meeting a Philosopher
Will, with arrogance say,
"There goes a fool."
But the Philosopher smiles sorrowfully,
With pity, and answers with humility:
"Thou hast said it."

There is a first seemingly, insignificant step
Unseen,
Unknown,
Which leads to Heaven or Hell.
It is at the point,
Where temptation has no string,—
Where life and death are synonymous.
It is at the point
Where we may turn future tears
Into future smiles.
It is at the point
Beyond which we are conditioned.
Beyond which,—as we say,—
We are in the hands of "Fate".

He who is wise but humble invites love and respect where a
fool has contempt and invites it.

The real wise man has sought all he knows from within himself; the intellectual man from others.

Man loses sight
Of that stupendous law of Progress.
He thinks Progress will not go on,
Without his egotistical activity;
And is startled into realization
Only when he sees himself engulfed
And strangled by the achievements
Of the younger generation,
Which ever settle about Old Age.

Measure your sanity
By how long your imagination
Can remain within the walls
Of common sense and reason.

He who will not be hungry
Cannot enjoy an appetite.
He who does not love
Cannot receive.
The only way to receive is to give.
He who gives, cleanses himself.
He who only takes, decays.
An empty room contains
The most fresh air.
A vacant nest has fulfilled
The purpose of Nature.
He who would be successful and happy
Let him do the labor he can do best,
And in his own way.
His individuality will place him
In his own sphere.
For we are all labelled, classified, ordained.
Or there would be no beginning,
Nor end,
Nor birth, nor death, in this life.
We all represent the symbol of time.
If you would gain knowledge
And be wise,
Learn from the tongues of babes and fools.
Instead of your wise men,
Who may know the sun's eclipses
Years in advance;
The distance of the stars,
And the name of every insect;
And who, in themselves are not happy,
And do not know love's companionship.
A child will teach you your needs.
A fool, what to avoid.

♠

It is easier to prevent a bruise than to heal one. Easier to prevent and control habits by education, than to cure them by sacrifice.

If you will remember the following it may solve some of your
    problems:
Does not today's food feed tomorrow's ambition?
Then why do you insist upon adding adulteration and flavors
To strangle your own special make of bread,
So that the owner of your borrowed flavor but claims his own,
As well as yours, to his credit.
Feed tomorrow's thought with your ambitions and ideals of yes-
    terday;
For those ideals are just what you are,
And may become what you long for most.
They are your choice of food when hungry, if you only know it.
Man's taste has been so abused, his desires so misshaped,
That he orders a big meal which is served too soon, or too late,
His unnatural desires having so much sway that there is no
    coordination in his entire system:
Then he bemoans his fate until Nature slows him down by force.
Be normal in all things;
For the deeper you sink in the ground the more labor,
And the less you find but materialism.
The higher you fly, the more mysterious clouds of spiritual
    fanaticism.
Still, both may produce a supermind.
But the happiest of the three is he who insists on walking on the
    surface of the earth,
With feet among the flowers, heart and head overlooking beauty
    and happiness.

You are ready to condemn the man who has made a mistake—
Is it because you envy,
But dare not make the same mistake
For want of an opportunity?
If not, where is your charity and tolerance, pity, and pride
For being stronger?

A fool can ask a question that a wise man cannot answer.
And if he could, the fool would not understand it.

The strong arm of the sculptor brings into existence the artist's greatest inspiration in the hardest marble.

His master-piece may then be lasting, and remembered and loved by future generations . .

Do you not think it is a law that he who is most valued must be visited by tragedies, tests of endurance, humiliation and sorrow?

Where is your quest?

Do you intend to rush heedlessly over numerous paths and by-paths, or will you remain in your own Soul poised and well-balanced?

You may have a light buggy in which you are going to ride around the world.

Are you not going to sit in the exact center of that buggy, realizing that the four wheels will carry you safely back home?

If you were to sit above one of the wheels only, it surely would be worn out before the other three.

And your mission would not be fulfilled.

Your quest would be in vain.

Common sense is in using every faculty of the brain.

Not riding to a judgment on one wheel . . .

Remain in the center of your Soul, where there is an answer to your quest.

It is not enough to possess power;
It is more essential
To know how to use it.
Do not envy one
Who displays it unwisely,
For he soon
Will be dispossessed of it,
As with one
Who possesses wealth unguarded.

A heart of gold has its many temptations—
More so than the heart of stone.

THERE ONCE WAS A MAN

Who was born in the depths of the valley of Nothingness.
He beheld the wonderful Sun in the heavens
That seemed to give life to all living things.
He made himself a vehicle, with a strong pair of tugs.
He loaded it with provisions and started up a mountain to be
    nearer this life-giving thing.

But the climb was difficult—a continuous pull on the tugs.
Every once in a while he came across the mistakes of others
Who like him endeavored to reach the top, but would slip and spill
    their load.
They would implore him to help them, in exchange for some of their
    goods.
And in the doing of this charity, his muscles became hard as steel;
Until at last he had reached the top, to behold the splendor at his
    feet.

But as he turned about, he was astonished
To behold a deep valley at his feet and a great mountain before him.
For he had but reached the top of a little foothill, called his mortal
    life.
Still he remained for a time, bathing himself in the glory of his
    achievements—
Until at last the sun went down.

Then the greatest Ambition was born—to climb the real mountain.
Still, how could he descend into the valley, and ascend the next?
For he realized that this side of the foothill mountain was as smooth
    as glass,
Where no one could ascend; nor once descended,
    could one stop his flight,
Because this was the valley of death.
Here his physical strength did him naught.
Still, realizing that the great load he had pulled up to the top
    would be capitalized with his momentum,
He prepared to descend.

By the help of his own deeds, and with the swiftness of lightning he
was carried down through oblivion.
And by the momentum was carried up to the great Mountain of
Compensation,
To the exact height of the foothill he had just left.
And there he stood, firm under foot,
And his passage paid for by his deeds and wisdom thus far adopted.

And now he possessed a continued want, which is the greatest
blessing on earth.
It is the pull of the compass, a definite fact,
The direct road to that place where intense activity becomes calm
and peaceful.

Nature gives birth to nothing to which it does not give sustenance
to exist,
And protection for a given time,
Of which to make use according to the understanding created by
experience.
The human body is the fertile ground
In which the roots of the soul make themselves known,
And as with the little colored flag of the plant, the blossom,
Introducing an individuality, and the coming of the fruit—
So it is with men and women.

What is pain
If not but a faithful voice of warning
Of disobedience to the laws of Nature
Under which we exist?

A cruel man uses anger
To avenge his cowardly blindness.
Bear in mind that often, if you don't do,
You can't.

Have you ever observed
How the needle of a a phonograph travels,
Touching every point of the record?
Why don't you do likewise,
With the opportunities of your territory,
Which is your record?
Why just keep in one depression,
Repeating over and over yesterday's activity,
Leaving out all the rest of your life's songs;
Then complain of its briefness,
Until someone else begins where you left off,
Only to place the flowers on your coffin
Because of songs unsung?
Wake up and sing them now.
Adjust the needle out of the same rut habit
And let the world know that God makes no mistake,
But that it is man only, who forgets
That which masters try to remind him of.
Is it not true?

One must concentrate upon his purpose,
Be it what it may,
Or make his mind receptive to inspiration
    upon a chosen subject only,
Or he may receive thoughts not essential,
    but detrimental to his development.

Grief and calamity are two of the finest whips
To bring us joy and success..

The Valley of the Pines

E VERY man is forced to exist or die. Then why not make your choice where you will live best; for contentment, not momentary pleasure with sorrow, despair and regrets?

One can choose his own flower pot to grow in, after leaving nature's great Hot-house: even to choosing those who may admire you and love you for just what you are.

I dare not tell you of what is really ahead of you.

If you knew you would stretch out your arms toward the blue sky, with tears in your eyes, and a longing in your heart to fly, to soar upward because of the distant beauty that is yours.

I have glimpsed that land of beauty.

And have been enamored by its magic.

But at times I dare not linger there, for fear of neglecting objectiveness.

If you do not labor for a purpose, you place no value on it.

For a thing, no matter how precious, is of no value unless you place it there yourself by what you would do to obtain it.

If you find and win the love of a woman, with but little effort, You will lose her to another, as easily as you won her.

But if it required half a lifetime, as in climbing a mountain to its height,

You will know the journey down, though more pleasant,

Has as many miles of road as going up.

So measure your *value* by what is required to obtain it.

Never profess to do more than you can.
The effort to maintain your assertion
Will be greater than the reward
From your deception.
With the same amount of energy
You could do better things
In your own way
The things that are yours to do.

When disputing over an opinion
Why not give your own
To match that of your opponent,
Rather than to produce none,
And only destroy his.
Why not give something in return
As a friendly bargain,
Instead of giving birth
To disappointed enemies.

You say you were never lost? But have you shown the way
to others? If not, then you ARE lost.

How could we exist,
Were it not for a purpose?
If we do not know that purpose
It should be our purpose to seek it,

Every man when lost
Must find himself
Or he will dispute
That he was ever lost
If someone else
Points out the right road.

Before considering being converted or initiated,
Do not accept the laws blindly.
You may buy that which you cannot support;
Obligate yourself to that which you cannot fulfill,
Breaking a law assumed without the sanction of your willingness
    and understanding,
Changing your entire makeup to obey the law of another;
Sinning for having broken a promise,
Assuming a law which will affect even your conscience,
Because that law seems to be an inspiration
Until you once find yourself in mental nakedness:
Then you will become its enemy
Instead of a tolerant human being.
Always be convinced logically and practically,
So there will be no residue of a soap bubble left
    to shame you.
How many martyrs have died in the past,
Convinced they died for a sacred Cause.
But we today call them fanatics, spies, traitors, revolutionists,
    "ahead of their times",
But nevertheless they were truly martyrs
Worthy of a crown and of their convictions.
Be sure your heart is with your mind,
Before you accept in haste
Anything that you intend to graft on your tree of life, So when it
bears fruit,
That branch will not hold fruit that will shame your own;
Though your own may be lemons (so essential to life),
And your adopted branch peaches—
God made nothing useless—
Not even the tail of a pig.

How could we exist,
Were it not for a purpose?
If we do not know that purpose
It should be our purpose to seek it,
Slowly but surely.

Nature has created our understanding
As the embryo of a chick,
Within an opaque shell.
So it might not, in its development
And involuntary growth,
Desire those things
Outside its own world.
This shell is opaque and brittle,
Until, by wisdom and knowing,
It becomes transparent.
Then knowledge removes
The superstitious potash,—
Brittleness,—
And makes it transparent,
And flexible,—to shape itself
According to its will and emotions.
Thus it is with ourselves.
As we evolve from ignorance and rigidity
Were we to see into the beyond,
We could not carry out the creation
Of our primitive worlds.
As we grow,
We tear away the veils,
Shaping ourselves according to the niche
We are destined to fill.
And only by degrees do we become aware
Of why our creation.
The purpose of all things we question.
But the Great Architect
Has placed life's answer
In every loving form.
And we could if we would,
Read the messages from the Father
To His self-Creating Sons.

Some men become famously wealthy,
Insisting on being in debt.

The scrubbing brush to a working woman
Is as important as the pen
To the President of the United States.
Never ridicule the flimsy bridge
You have just passed over.
You may have to use it
On your return trip.

If environments cannot be altered, it is well to have a few apparent calamities so that under the law of relativity, one is made to give more value to that which has become commonplace by familiarity.

The greatest sorrow and tragedy in life
Comes to those who seek happiness at the end of the trail
Rather than in the making of the trail.

If you wish to hold
What you think is yours,
Be sure that it is paid for.
And by your own coin.
Remembering, incidentally,
That each penny represents its value in deeds.
Or your possession is but a debt.

If you interest yourself in the roots of a rose, the blossom will be interested in you.

He who wins friends by frankness
Holds them without flattery.

If personality is good salesmanship,
Then the salesman
Must have sold himself the facts
Enough to believe them absolutely
To convince the buyer of the facts.
Then why not convince teachers and missionaries
To convince themselves first,
Before trying to convince others
Of that which they themselves have certain doubts:
At least enough so to be sold by those
Who do believe, even though they may be mistaken.
At least there will be some
Who will be entirely convinced of facts
By the mistakes made by him
Who did believe, and still was mistaken
Be sure you outlive your apprenticeship
Before assuming mastership—
Or some pupil
May hail you as an equal
To your embarrassment among masters.

Always be yourself.
Then you'll know what you are,
And what you can be.

If you wish the world to follow you,
Keep on walking alone without looking back.
And when you have reached your goal
A multitude will be at your back.

Miracles are not so convincing as the fruits of them.
Christ did not convince the leaders of His time,
But the fruits of His work convinced the world.

Prevent rather than cure
By studying not only that which you're thinking with
But the material you have with which to shape that which does
    your thinking.
For your state of mind can be what you will it to be
By the right purpose in willing.

Learn how to forget what you should, or will,
As well as to remember that which again may be born to you
    beneficially,
So as to correct that mistake you ought to forget in its correction.

When you ridicule another,
You have been blinded by the same vice in a new form
As that of which you accuse your victim.
Just as he fails to understand his own knowledge of wisdom,
Or he whose physical strength makes him arrogant
Only to be humiliated by one who may be weak
      but not aware of it.

How many people fear to lose their good living
By leaving their hypocrisy behind?
Who advocates truth so that nobody may question his sincerity
Nor expose him to ridicule because of lack of truth?

    Our bad habits make us prisoners, and our false pride is the
jailer that keeps us there.

You are what you are; but can be what you will.

    We always lose sight of what we've got, in our efforts to obtain
what we haven't got.

When adversity comes, it is a sign that we are given a test, or given work to to.
The Masters test only those whom they feel to be worth while, so as to be sure of results.

If you have found some truth,
Don't get over-excited and brag about it,
Or you my be checked up
To prove how ignorant you have been.
Rather add it to your stock of knowledge
For it is then already accepted,
And your word is law,
For that is truth.

Thoughts are bound to escape that may be injurious.
Your tongue of ill-reproof is evidence of that.
Think twice, for and against,
Before you think of thoughts you intend to express

Do well, and conquer your work,
However menial,
And you will have done
What Christ did,
When He died upon the Cross.
And for the same purpose.

Sit down and meditate · from within, a new world shall be born, in place of. what you are forced to accept.

If you lose yourself in serving men, God will find you to be served.

If you can't think it out, you can't act it out.

Each Individual must keep his balance if he wishes to succeed and
  be happy.
And always under some good discipline
To adopt a personal mental control governed by logic, reason and
  justice.

When the time comes that the public may know and realize
what supposedly great men think about instead of what they talk
about, you will behold a welcome miracle in the adjustment of man-
made laws as influenced by Godmade laws.

Don't think for a moment
That you can always get away
With those things that you try to prevent others from
  getting away with.

Misfortune only follows when we starve our intuition,
Or follow the dictates of another into slavery.

A person who does not improve things is not improving himself.

Did you ever try to change your mind when angry?
Try it, and see what you are made of.
Don't lock up your reason when it is needed more.
When you start in to lick a man,
Notice if it is the same man you hit with your first blow.

As you climb the mountain to successs, be sure to look down periodically, as you do upward.
It will make you more cautious and sure of your worthiness.
It will show you from what rank you came, and to what depths
  you may fall.

Many a man has been forced to great deeds, who capitalizes un-
earned reward,
While many a worthy martyr died in obscurity
To have his name and deeds resurrected in the selfish display of
glory
That might have saved him to us in untold wisdom.
Far rather sustain life and receive living food for knowledge
Than only his dead memory of words, with no reply.
The world looks big to little men.
The world is small to big men.

Many an educated man becomes a fool through a leaky tongue.
Many an ocean liner sinks by a slow leak because too insignificant
to notice such magnitude.
Still, a drop of kerosene in five gallons of milk manifests itself.
Let him who is always so ready to dispute the things of the spirit
Deny the existence of the evaporated brandy that he ran through
his leaky still,
And when evaporated into the air—
Ask him where it is.
Or have him color a glass full of alcohol;
And later when he finds the glass empty, and only the color
remaining,
Ask him where it is—
And if it is not a fact that had he placed his glass full of alcohol
in an air-tight room,
He would have found it condensed on the floor,
To prove that the thing he could not see after it left the glass, was
still there.
Likewise with spiritual things.

The Valley of the Pines

IT is better and safer to shape and build your cocoon with your own hands and material,
  Instead of borrowing from your thoughtless neighbor
Who not only needs his own material but gives you what is unfit
    for your protection—
Providing you expect the wings to carry you from the blossom of
    achievements to the fruits of understanding.

Because you think you have no chance to make good,
Don't give up;
For who told you that anyone was better than you are
If you did not make comparison
With someone you thought greater than you?
Why not let them
Really compare their achievements with yours
And see where you stand?
And then, if they were in your place,
Where really is the goal
That you both are travelling for?
Just wait until you both get inside
Of the bright lights of the City,
And let's see the paces of both of you.
That is the time you make your speed.
And there are more country miles than city miles.
So come on and "click."

Forget past failures by remembering future possibilities.

We are just what we are
And can make ourselves what we intend to
If our intentions are sincere.
A man without a want
Is a ship without a rudder or compass.
And a man with a real want
Has already sensed
The laurel leaves of Victory;
Has already inhaled the fragrant rose
Of the seed he is about to plant.
And if I am able to do this,
Then every human being is able to do likewise
For we are all constituted alike.
We all possess the seven prismatic colors with which to paint
  Nature.
We all possess the seven notes of music
So that we may sing and hear.
We all live through the seven epochs of
Seven years each of life.
And we labor six days in the week, to rest
Upon the seventh.
And we sit outdoors after a terrific storm
To behold the rainbow of seven colors
That tries to teach us of its message
Which was created for man and woman alone.
How futile it would be for an artist to create
A masterpiece with a primary color lacking;
For a musician to interpret life
With only three notes.
And it is thus with those who have failed.
They have failed to find
And make use of the seven opportunities
Which they possess.

Intuitive people think the same thoughts. It is neither coincidence nor telepathy when two radios, attuned to the same broadcast, play the same tune.

We have no right to starve our emotions.
We have need of them all
If only to counteract certain resultant evils.
But if you would succeed as you should
Be sure to hire a caretaker
For each emotion that manifests itself
Above normal.

Most people seldom drink from their own springs of Inspiration.
They drink from their neighbor's stagnant pool of waste,
Allowing their own spring of running water—
The water of life—to dry up.
Our own spring of water
Will flow only when we use the water
And when the mouth of the spring is kept clean
And clear of debris.
By wrong thinking we merely exist.
By right thinking we drink of the pure waters of life.

When a good soldier kneels to pray
Before the battle,
He does not expect God's legions
To fight his battle.
He expects to be inspired
By the sense of justice—
And then, himself, to do the fighting
That is required of him.

It is well to endure a little sorrow, to give birth to pity, sympathy, mercy, charity and love.

Sit down and meditate; from within, a new world shall be born—in place of what you have been forced to accept.

I would rather make keys to unlock doors
Than locks to lock them.
The man who locks up riches is in danger of losses always.
He who makes keys can look forward to profits.
He encourages production, honesty, circulation and progress.
The man who locks up riches, does so only for self-gratification,
Which encourages men to become dishonest, covetous, selfish and
    criminal.
If we think we have the most perfect metal, or organization, and
    hoard it up,
How can there be improvements?
If preventive measures are used, why not encourage even the beg-
    gar to give up his mental secrets to mankind,
Instead of making a criminal of him by discouragement.
Give every man a chance, and he will make or break imself,
And not be only a beggar,
But either a man or nothing at all.

Many a child is lost on the broad sea of life by the mother's selfish
    love,
Depriving her child of that compass of free action and search for
    self-reliance,
That only means wreckage of slavery when that mother passes on
    with that compass—her child's individuality.

Man, in idleness, makes food for his master,
Losing sight of its mission
Which, far from being ornamental,
Is to be a necessity in his activity.

Is it not gratifying to rest?
But how can one enjoy rest if he is not tired?
How become honestly tired without labor?
And why labor without reward?
And how can one accept reward without earning it,
When it must be paid for in full?

Try to live so that the *unseen world* may have more respect for you than those who flatter you, in order to forget your virtues and make you forget their sins.

If indeed the sparrows's fall is recorded
Then the prayer of a child of God
Will surely reach on High
And be answered,
Even though the answer comes
At the pace of a snail.

It is the green lithe limb that bends before the wind of adversity,
When the proud, stiff limb refuses, and is torn off.

When I go into a church, I make-belive the Master is there.
And then I don't ask him for anything.
I thank him for what I have.

Are things worthwhile?
Then make yourself a part of those things with which you wish
to be identified.
And they cannot exist with you.

Condemnation, ridicule and envy are always made use of
In trying to prevent a real man from climbing the ladder of success.

It is often your superfluous energy that gets you into trouble:
Your extra money to gamble, into problems.
So make good use of it by controlling the impulse of extravagence.
waste, and mere chance.

It is as we cast our bread upon the waters
That counts,
And not the returns we expect to get.
We are paid for each kind act or deed,
The gold is at the end of the rainbow.
But think not at all of the earnings,
Beware of spiritual greed.
And in a mad race let us not dissipate
Our strength indiscreetly
And be prevented from furthering the greater work.
Some are called to be sheep,
Some are called to be shepherds,
Some hunger—others feed.
But though we are asked for bread,
We must also eat and drink
That our strength may sustain us
To fulfil the law of evolution
And that we may tread the road
Leading to Eternity.
And then will the rainbow
Be a halo about the head
Of a Child of God.

The following page contains a list of
the publications of
THE GREAT SCHOOL OF NATURAL SCIENCE

LITERATURE OF THE GREAT SCHOOL
OF NATURAL SCIENCE...

THE GREAT MESSAGE $4.00
  *The Lineal Key of The Great
  School of the Masters*

THE GREAT WORK $4.00
  *The Constructive Principle of
  Nature in Individual Life.*

> J. E. Richardson

THE GREAT KNOWN $4.00
  *What Science Knows of
  the Spiritual World.*

THE GREAT PSYCHOLOGICAL CRIME $4.00
  *The Destructive Principle of
  Nature in Individual Life.*

HARMONICS OF EVOLUTION, Florence Huntley $4.00
  *The Struggle for Happiness, and Individual Completion
  Through Polarity or Affinity.*

THE BROTHERHOOD OF MAN, by J. E. Richardson . . $2.50

SELF-UNFOLDMENT, Vol. 1, 2, J E Richardson . . . ea. $3.00

WHO ANSWERS PRAYER? PO, RA, TK $2.00

TO YOU (Magazine) . . . . . { per year . $3.00
                            { single copy   50

RELIGIOUS SANITY, by A. R. Jackson . $2.50

THE ROAD TO HARMONIOUS LIVING
  by "Student of Life" $1.00

HOW TO RELAX . . . . 2 for 25

QUESTIONS AND ANSWERS ON NATURAL SCIENCE . . . $3.00

(California Residents Please Add 4% Sales Tax)

PIONEER PRESS
25,355 Spanish Ranch Road
LOS GATOS, CALIFORNIA

THE GREAT MESSAGE

by

J. E. RICHARDSON TK

Vol. V
Harmonic Series

This inspiring book is an introduction to the findings of The Great School of the Masters The Great School is that great Central Source and Reservoir of Knowledge (Religious, Philosophical, Moral, Physical, Spiritual and Psychical) which the best intelligences of all ages have intuitively sensed and definitely accepted as the great beneficent, constructive, uplifting and progressive influence in the Evolution of Mankind from Spiritual Infancy and Darkness to Soul Maturity and Illumination

The records of The Great School contain a detailed account of the Life and Work of the Master Jesus. To this school He went for His spiritual instruction In it He spent the years of His special preparation From it He went forth to preach the Gospel of Peace on Earth and the Kingdom of Love. For the cause it represents, He labored and suffered and died.

Besides our own Master Jesus, there were numerous other Masters, who were commissioned by The Great School to bring its Message of Life, Light and Immortality to the world Some of the most well known are, Confucius, Zarathustra, Buddha, Moses, Krishna, Eliola, Pythagoras and Melchizedek.

The pathway of The Great School of the Masters is again open to true seekers after Truth, and the duly and truly prepared, worthy and well qualified may find the way to its Temple of Light and without money and without price receive such knowledge as they may merit

A modern movement known as The Great School of Natural Science has been launched by the Great Parent School of the Masters to give to the Progressive Intelligence of the twentieth century a definite and scientific presentation of *THE PHILOSOPHY OF INDIVIDUAL LIFE* as taught by its members throughout all the past ages.

Those who find in THE GREAT MESSAGE an inspiration to seek further Light will have a new and broader outlook on life, and renewed zeal to make the most of it. The door to the Temple of Wisdom is ajar

$4 00

CPSIA information can be obtained
at www.ICGtesting.com
Printed in the USA
BVHW042152270921
617665BV00010B/226